P9-CKD-867

Back Back Back

by Itamar Moses

A SAMUEL FRENCH ACTING EDITION

SAMUEL FRENCH

FOUNDED 1830

NEW YORK HOLLYWOOD LONDON TORONTO

SAMUELFRENCH.COM

Copyright © 2009 by Itamar Moses

ALL RIGHTS RESERVED

CAUTION: Professionals and amateurs are hereby warned that *BACK BACK BACK* is subject to a royalty. It is fully protected under the copyright laws of the United States of America, the British Commonwealth, including Canada, and all other countries of the Copyright Union. All rights, including professional, amateur, motion picture, recitation, lecturing, public reading, radio broadcasting, television and the rights of translation into foreign languages are strictly reserved. In its present form the play is dedicated to the reading public only.

The amateur live stage performance rights to *BACK BACK BACK* are controlled exclusively by Samuel French, Inc., and royalty arrangements and licenses must be secured well in advance of presentation. PLEASE NOTE that amateur royalty fees are set upon application in accordance with your producing circumstances. When applying for a royalty quotation and license please give us the number of performances intended, dates of production, your seating capacity and admission fee. Royalties are payable one week before the opening performance of the play to Samuel French, Inc., at 45 W. 25th Street, New York, NY 10010.

Royalty of the required amount must be paid whether the play is presented for charity or gain and whether or not admission is charged.

Stock royalty quoted upon application to Samuel French, Inc.

For all other rights than those stipulated above, apply to: SUBIAS, One Union Square West, No. 913, New York, NY 10003, Attn: Mark Subias.

Particular emphasis is laid on the question of amateur or professional readings, permission and terms for which must be secured in writing from Samuel French, Inc.

Copying from this book in whole or in part is strictly forbidden by law, and the right of performance is not transferable.

Whenever the play is produced the following notice must appear on all programs, printing and advertising for the play: "Produced by special arrangement with Samuel French, Inc."

Due authorship credit must be given on all programs, printing and advertising for the play.

ISBN 978-0-573-69612-1   Printed in U.S.A.   #4773

No one shall commit or authorize any act or omission by which the copyright of, or the right to copyright, this play may be impaired.

No one shall make any changes in this play for the purpose of production.

Publication of this play does not imply availability for performance. Both amateurs and professionals considering a production are strongly advised in their own interests to apply to Samuel French, Inc., for written permission before starting rehearsals, advertising, or booking a theatre.

No part of this book may be reproduced, stored in a retrieval system, or transmitted in any form, by any means, now known or yet to be invented, including mechanical, electronic, photocopying, recording, videotaping, or otherwise, without the prior written permission of the publisher.

IMPORTANT BILLING AND CREDIT REQUIREMENTS

All producers of *BACK BACK BACK must* give credit to the Author of the Play in all programs distributed in connection with performances of the Play, and in all instances in which the title of the Play appears for the purposes of advertising, publicizing or otherwise exploiting the Play and/or a production. The name of the Author *must* appear on a separate line on which no other name appears, immediately following the title and *must* appear in size of type not less than fifty percent of the size of the title type.

In addition the following credit *must* be given in all programs and publicity information distributed in association with this piece:

World Premiere at the Old Globe, San Diego, California, Louis G. Spisto, CEO/Executive Producer, Jerry Patch, Co-Artistic Director, Darko Tresnjak, Co-Artistic Director.

Originally produced in New York by the Manhattan Theatre Club, Lynne Meadow, Artistic Director, Barry Grove Executive Producer.

BACK BACK BACK premiered at The Old Globe, San Diego on September 19, 2008; Louis G. Spisto, Executive Director, Jerry Patch, Co-Artistic Director, Darko Tresnjak, Co-Artistic Director.

DIRECTOR: Davis McCallum
SCENIC DESIGN: Lee Savage
COSTUME DESIGN: Christal Weatherly
LIGHTING DESIGN: Russell Champa
SOUND DESIGN: Paul Peterson
STAGE MANAGER: Tracy Skoczelas

CAST:

KENT... Brendan Griffin
RAUL.....................................Joaquin Perez-Campbell
ADAM .... Nick Mills

BACK BACK BACK opened at Manhattan Theatre Club in New York City on October 30, 2008; Lynne Meadow, Artistic Director, Barry Grove, Executive Producer.

DIRECTOR: Daniel Aukin
SCENIC AND COSTUME DESIGN: David Zinn
LIGHTING DESIGN: David Weiner
SOUND DESIGN: Daniel Baker, Ryan Rumery
PRODUCTION STAGE MANAGER: Kasey Ostopchuck
STAGE MANAGER: Kyle R. Gates

CAST:

KENT...Jeremy Davidson
RAUL...James Martinez
ADAM ....Michael Mosley

CHARACTERS

KENT
RAUL
ADAM

A NOTE ABOUT SCENE HEADINGS: The momentum of the play depends partly on the audience being made aware, at the top of each scene, how far we've moved in both time and space since the previous scene. What this means is somehow using the headings that appear in the text for each of the nine scenes as an explicit part of the transitions between them. The best way to do this, probably, is to use some type of scoreboard on which the headings can appear, and then remain visible, such that they gradually line up like the recorded outcomes of each of the nine innings of a game. But, short of that, some way of conveying up front, at minimum, both what month and year we're in, and our location geographically, as a sort of button on each transition, is desirable.

A NOTE ABOUT NUDITY: It is not necessary for the actor playing Raul to be completely naked at any point during scenes 3 or 4. Nudity is, of course, an option, but would be, at that moment, needlessly distracting, in the opinion of the author.

1.
August 1984
Southern California

(A press room in the Olympic Village. KENT is talking to the press. Perhaps he is seated at a table at a microphone. He is wearing a Team USA baseball uniform.)

KENT. Well, geez. Um, honestly? We're not even thinking about that, we're not even paying attention to that. We're not here to talk about the past, the politics of it, or the behind the scenes drama, or the negative, we're just here to play our game. Because, first of all, it's just an honor and a privilege even just to be here, to be playing with this great bunch of guys, in a situation that really is an honor, against all these other countries, who are just being great to us, um, I mean, they're our guests, but you know what I mean, everybody's getting along just great, and we're glad to be playing well, which, I mean, nobody's exactly surprised, this is our sport, and our home turf, so I guess that we, you know, did come in with some expectations that we would do well, but everybody, Thrill, and Larkin, and everyone, we're obviously pretty pumped, pretty psyched, that we were able to meet those, you know, expectations, and we're pretty psyched, pretty pumped, to be out of the elimination rounds, and into the semis where it counts, though, then again, it is, you know, we are still a demonstration sport, sure, or, what do they call it, like, an exhibition, or whatever, as opposed to like a full-on medal event, which, okay, they've got guys getting medals for how far they can throw a log, but baseball is somehow this big issue for some reason? I don't get it. *(beat)* Oh, but, I don't know, as to a boycott, or whatever, like I said, to be honest, nobody's giving it all that much thought. Definitely not here on the baseball club. That's not even cluttering up our minds, we're just gonna keep doing what we've been doing, keep being positive, and try to win this thing. And, uh, not get a medal for it. *(beat)* It's South Korea in the semis, right? We're gonna kick their ass.

2.
October 1988
Southern California

(A weight room. RAUL *is lying on the bench press. He is wearing the workout clothes of a major league baseball team. He sits up. Looks at his watch. Lies back down. Moments pass.* ADAM *enters, wearing the uniform of the same team.)*

ADAM. Hey.

RAUL. The fuck took you so long? *(He sits up. Sees who it is.)* Oh. Hey, Adam.

ADAM. Sorry, I, uh… Just. I thought there'd be…

(A moment. ADAM *turns to go.)*

RAUL. Hey, hey, no, it's no problem. I just… What's up, rook?

ADAM. Nothing.

RAUL. *(sudden enthusiasm)* Hey! Back to back to back, baby! Wooooo!

ADAM. Oh, hey, no –

RAUL. Oh yeah! Back to back to back, baby! Wooooo!

ADAM. They haven't even announced it yet. We don't even know.

RAUL. Yeah, no, you're right, you're right. *(beat)*

ADAM. So –

RAUL. Back to back to back, baby! Wooooo!

ADAM. Stop it, Raul. Seriously.

RAUL. What's the *matter* with you, *Adam.*

ADAM. Nothing! Just. I was actually looking for a place to be alone. Get my head clear for the game.

RAUL. And you came to the weight room?

ADAM. Most of the guys on the team don't lift.

RAUL. That is true.

ADAM. Yeah.

RAUL. Their loss.

ADAM. I guess. *(pause)* But so. I just, uh... That's all.

RAUL. Okay.

*(Pause. **ADAM** doesn't go anywhere.)*

RAUL. Is there something I can do for you?

ADAM. Uh. No. No, no, no.

RAUL. Okay.

ADAM. Just. I don't feel great.

RAUL. Oh.

ADAM. I mean, it's nerves, it's just nerves, but I do feel kinda antsy. Anxious. But I'm fine. *(pause)* It's nerves. I feel a little nervous. And I'm like sweating a lot. And I'm having a hard time keeping my hands still. But I'm cool. *(pause)* And I feel maybe like I'm gonna pass out, or throw up, or first one and then the other, but like I don't know in what order. And I don't want Tony to see me like this because then he'll completely lose faith in me as a player.

RAUL. Um. Okay.

ADAM. Yeah. So.

RAUL. You had a great year. You'll be fine.

ADAM. Well, yeah, no, I know. I know. *(pause)* I didn't feel this way during the year, though, is the thing.

RAUL. Well we've got a big game tonight.

ADAM. I know.

RAUL. Game One. And we're in their house. And they've got their ace on the hill. And we've gotta set the tone for the whole series, rook. Tonight.

ADAM. I know. I think that's probably what it is, too.

RAUL. No what I mean is you should get your head straight because we need you.

ADAM. Oh. *(beat)* I mean, yeah. I know.

RAUL. Because a big part of this game? Is *mental.* You know?

ADAM. I know that, Raul.

RAUL. I mean you gotta be *in* it. Up *here.*

ADAM. I know what you mean, Raul.

RAUL. Yeah but so my point is, sure, you had a great season, but also you need to deliver when it counts. In the post-season. Which is now. So –

ADAM. Have *you* ever been in the post-season – ?

RAUL. *(overlapping)* Let me answer your question with a question. Am I shaking and sweating and about to hurl like some kind of an amateur pussy? The answer to that question? Is no. I am calm. Fired up even. How did I do in the A.L.C.S., Adam? I kicked ass. And I cannot wait to step into the box against this guy tonight, this, uh… What's his name?

ADAM. Hershiser.

RAUL. *(with faux innocence)* Right, but, uh. What Hershiser?

ADAM. *(oblivious to the set-up)* Orel.

RAUL. Heh heh. I know.

ADAM. What? Oh.

RAUL. *(overlapping)* Who names their kid "Orel"? I mean…! That's just cruel! "Orel."

ADAM. How would you feel if someone made fun of your name, Raul?

RAUL. I would tell them it's the Spanish variant of the Old Norse Raoulfi meaning Counsel of the Wolf. *(beat)* As I was saying, I am not afraid of, uh, of Orel… Heh. Heh. Sorry. It's just –

ADAM. Please continue.

RAUL. Oh! Hey. That reminds me. And you'll like this. *This* you'll like. After the game? There's this *ridiculous* girl I want you to meet. *Ridiculous.* She's friends with this other chick I'm kind of involved with, or who I get, like, reinvolved with again whenever we come down to L.A.? And, actually, I was *kind of* involved with both of them? But not really the second one. But I *can* tell you? That she really likes baseball players. Like. She really *really* likes them. Like. Really a *lot.*

ADAM. *(beat)* That's fantastic, Raul. Thanks.

RAUL. The fuck is wrong with you?

ADAM. Just…! *(beat)* Nothing. Nothing. That will really be great after the game.

RAUL. Yeah. You're right. It will.

ADAM. I…! *(beat)* Maybe I should just tell Tony. See if he wants to sit me down.

RAUL. What?

ADAM. If, since, because I don't want to, like, hurt the team!

RAUL. Yeah but that would be pretty humiliating for you to have to sit one out in a clutch situation. It would be hard to come back from that.

ADAM. Well you know what? You, like, *riding* me about it? And, like, offering me your leftover *tail*? Isn't helping.

RAUL. Oh! Oh. You, uh… You want my help?

ADAM. I, uh…! Why do you think I'm *talking* to you?

RAUL. If you wanted help why didn't you say so, Adam?

ADAM. I'm a professional athlete. It can be hard for us to just ask.

RAUL. Well you're in luck. Because I can help you. I mean. I can help you help yourself. In a big way. If, uh. If you're really sure that you want my help.

ADAM. Uhh… *(beat)* Is there something in particular you're trying to say? Because if there is then I'm not getting it.

RAUL. *(pause)* Come here. Spot me for a minute.

(ADAM goes over to the bench press.)

ADAM. It's weird that you and Kent get away with this.

RAUL. Um. With what?

ADAM. Working out with weights.

RAUL. Oh.

ADAM. With lifting. Tony doesn't like it.

RAUL. That's true. He doesn't.

ADAM. He says it's bad for you.

RAUL. That's right. He does.

ADAM. But you guys just go ahead and do it anyway.

RAUL. Sure. I mean, he can make his demands, and yell, but the fuck is Tony gonna do really? We're his stars. Without us he doesn't –

(KENT enters, also wearing the team workout clothes.)

KENT. Sorry. Media. *(beat)* Oh. Adam. Hey.

ADAM. Hey, Kent.

(ADAM moves away from the bench press, clearing space for KENT to take up the spotting position. RAUL points among the three of them.)

RAUL. Hey! Back to back to back, baby! Wooooo!

KENT. Oh did they announce?

ADAM. No. No. They haven't even *voted.* Not until the season is over.

KENT. Right. That's what I thought.

RAUL. Well, yeah, but come on, Kent, I mean, you sort of get a general sense before that, right? I mean, my year, I pretty much knew a month before. And, last year, same for you, right?

KENT. I guess. People are always kind of informally polling each other or whatever so there can be a vague idea of what's going to go down pretty far in advance sometimes, which, um, what is so funny, Raul?

(Because RAUL has been chuckling.)

RAUL. Heh. "Polling each other."

KENT. Yeah that's great.

ADAM. Well, whatever, now I'm probably not even gonna get it now and I'll feel extra stupid because you got me all pumped up and then it didn't happen.

RAUL. See? This is what I'm talking about! This mentality you've got going mentally up there is just totally fucking with you!

KENT. Hey, lay off! Rook's trying to get focused.

RAUL. Rook is ready to pass out and vomit.

KENT. What?

RAUL. Tell him.

ADAM. Thanks, Raul, that's awesome.

KENT. You okay?

ADAM. Yeah, I'm fine, I'm fine, it's just nerves, I'm just a little nervous.

RAUL. And?

ADAM. And…! Like sweaty and shaky and nauseous. And light-headed

KENT. Wow. Maybe you should, uh, maybe you should tell Tony, have him sit you down, if –

RAUL. Great. That's great advice.

KENT. What? I'm just saying if the team –

RAUL. He has an opportunity to play on the big stage and he's spooked and you're instantly telling him to sit it out? Why don't you try for like a half a second to help him get it together?

KENT. *(to ADAM)* Um. Okay. Have you tried taking some deep breaths?

RAUL. Deep breaths? That's your advice?

KENT. What.

RAUL. *I* offered to get him laid.

ADAM. Jesus. You guys? I'm *fine.*

KENT. Okay, but, seriously. Just, like, try to slow down your heart rate and get calm and slow your pulse and just take deep even breaths. Okay?

ADAM. Okay.

KENT. *(to RAUL)* You ready to lift?

RAUL. Aw, already, really? Yeah that'd be nice.

KENT. Like I said. Press wanted quotes.

(During the following, KENT spots RAUL for a set. ADAM attempts to take deep breaths off to one side.)

RAUL. *(lifting)* I hate talking to those guys. It's a total mind-fuck. It's like they already know what they want to say about everything, and then they just take whatever you say and make it, like, fit into what they were going to say already.

KENT. Don't talk while you're lifting.

RAUL. *(lifting)* Oh because you're the expert on condition-ing now?

KENT. No, just –

RAUL. *(lifting)* Because in fact, *Kent,* if I am lifting at a level that is comfortable for me I should be able to talk comfortably while I lift.

(**RAUL** *is finished with his set. He sits up. He stares at* **KENT.** *A beat.*)

KENT. You're right.

RAUL. I know I am.

KENT. Well you are.

RAUL. Good. I know.

(**KENT** *and* **RAUL** *switch places.* **KENT** *does a set.* **RAUL** *spots him. Meanwhile:*)

RAUL. In fact, this debate about conditioning is not unre-lated to what I was talking to you about just a moment ago, Adam.

ADAM. What? What.

RAUL. About how to help you help yourself in a way other than telling you to breath or to somehow magically slow down your own pulse.

ADAM. Oh.

RAUL. Because you know what the secret to conditioning is? Or, what the thing is that gets in people's way the most when they work out?

KENT. *(lifting)* Hey –

RAUL. *(to* **KENT***)* Don't talk, Kent. *(to* **ADAM***)* Do you know?

ADAM. No.

RAUL. People think it's how much weight you can lift, or how many reps you can do, or something like that, but it's not, that's not what it is.

ADAM. It's not.

RAUL. No.

(**KENT** *has finished his set. He sits up.*)

KENT. Raul —

RAUL. Just a second, Kent. The biggest thing that gets in your way? Is recovery time. By which I mean the *time* that it takes you to *recover*.

KENT. He knows what recovery time means.

RAUL. *(to* ADAM*)* Is this helping?

ADAM. Yes.

RAUL. Actual information that's not some zen bullshit is helpful?

ADAM. Yeah.

RAUL *(to* KENT*)* So shut up, Kent.

KENT. *(gesturing)* Yeah, but, just, come on, could we —

(KENT *and* RAUL *switch places. During which:)*

RAUL. Like if you maybe do a set for a particular muscle group and you have to rest a while before you do the next set? That's way more limiting than amount or reps or anything.

KENT. Are you gonna go or what?

RAUL. In a second. *(to* ADAM*)* Or if you do a whole routine for a whole bunch of muscle groups and have to wait a day, two days, before you do that routine again. But if your recovery time was lower, then instead of rotating through, you know, chest, legs, back, arms, whatever, and you could just go arms, arms, arms…! And that's the biggest obstacle. Which is something that not a lot of people know.

ADAM. *(He feels unwell.)* Ohhh.

RAUL. And the best thing you could do is find a way to eliminate that problem.

ADAM. Oh, god, I don't feel good.

RAUL. And it turns out? That there is one.

ADAM. What is wrong with me?

RAUL. Hey. Do what you gotta do. The bathroom's right back there.

ADAM. No, I'm fine. I'm fine. *(pause)* Yeah. I think I'm fine. What were you saying? *(pause)* I'm fine. Go on.

RAUL. You sure?

ADAM. Yeah, just...

RAUL. I was saying –

ADAM. Oh fuck. Oh god.

> (**ADAM** *runs off.*)

RAUL. *(calling off, after him)* You do what you gotta do!

> (**KENT** *is staring at* **RAUL.** **RAUL.** *is oblivious. A moment.*)

RAUL. So it's, uh, is it my turn to – ?

KENT. The hell are you doing.

RAUL. What.

KENT. "The best thing you could do is find a way to eliminate that problem?"

RAUL. Oh, come on, relax, okay?

KENT. I'm totally relaxed. I just think that you should leave him alone. *(beat)*

RAUL. What?

KENT. You heard what I said.

RAUL. Okay. I see. And...is that an order?

KENT. What? No.

RAUL. Oh, see, because, here I was thinking that you were sitting over there just fucking *telling* me what I could and couldn't do –

KENT. Hey, come on –

RAUL. But now I see that I was wrong. Which is good. That's good. Because I'd hate to think that just because you're everybody's can't-do-shit-wrong fucking golden boy over there, Tony in your fucking pocket, that that somehow means you can tell me what to do. I would hate to think *that.*

KENT. You don't have to be a dick about it.

RAUL. *You* don't have to be a fucking dick about it.

KENT. It's just, I think, getting him caught up in it. Might be a little misguided.

RAUL. What does that mean?

KENT. What. *(beat)* What "misguided"?

RAUL. Yeah.

KENT. It…! There's risks, there's some risks, and I don't think you should bring him into it. I don't think you should do that to him.

RAUL. I'm not going to do anything *to* him. Kent. He asked me for help. And I'm going to make clear to him some options he may not have thought about.

KENT. Well you have a way of talking about options that makes a guy feel like if he doesn't take those options then that means that he's stupid.

RAUL. I think that anyone who doesn't take *this* option *is* stupid.

KENT. Um. Exactly.

RAUL. *(mock concern)* Whoa. Uh-oh. Hey now. Did I make *you* feel stupid?

KENT. What? Fuck you. No. *You* did not make *me* feel stupid.

RAUL. Oh! Now. What is *that* supposed to mean?

KENT. Nothing. Just. I think you should leave him alone.

RAUL. Huh.

KENT. That's all.

RAUL. Mm. *(beat)* See, it's funny, because when I did the same thing for you, I didn't exactly hear you complain or even really have any doubts.

KENT. Okay, well, first of all, I don't do it like you do it.

RAUL. Uh. *What?*

KENT. Just, I'm just saying, I just do my thing, that I do, but I don't do your whole like big regimen, or routine, or whatever, the way *you* do it.

RAUL. Oh, so there's, like, *levels* of it now, that are okay, or not okay – ?

KENT. But, whatever, apart from that, it makes *sense* for me.

RAUL. It does.

KENT. Yeah.

RAUL. But it doesn't for him.

KENT. No.

RAUL. No?

KENT. No it does not make sense for him.

RAUL. Because you're the expert now.

KENT. No, I just –

RAUL. One year, one year and you're the expert, who should do it, who shouldn't, dispensing it from your locker, with your little lab coat on, hey, everybody come see Doctor K, he knows what amounts are okay and not okay, he knows what makes *sense*.

KENT. *(overlapping, on "dispensing")* No. No. No. Would you...! I'm just saying I don't think that it's necessarily for everybody! And you're a leader and you're a star and he's gonna listen to you!

RAUL. Well he should listen to me because I'm the one that knows what I'm talking about because I've thought about it and figured it out for years, since I was in the minors, and I'm not some guy who just got into it like a half a second ago who's acting now like he invented it!

KENT. I'm not. I'm just...saying.

RAUL. Yeah. I heard you.

KENT. Okay. That's all. *(beat)* So, go, come on, it's –

RAUL. And what the fuck does that mean it's not for everybody?

KENT. Uh. I just think that it's not.

RAUL. Why not.

KENT. I think it's pretty obvious.

RAUL. Pretend I'm a fucking moron.

KENT. Uh. Because, sure, the extra power is great, and it's not a problem if you play a position where it's okay to have that bulk, but...

RAUL. But?

KENT. Adam's not camped out in deep right.

RAUL. I know that. He plays third base.

KENT. He... What? No he doesn't.

RAUL. Or, I mean –

KENT. Tony moved him.

RAUL. When?

KENT. Like six months ago!

RAUL. You know, it's hard to see who's where from back there, I –

KENT. He's playing second! He's right in front to you!

RAUL. Okay. So?

KENT. So he needs to be fast.

RAUL. Uh-huh.

KENT. And he needs to get the ball off quick. To me.

RAUL. Right.

KENT. And he hits for average. Not for power.

RAUL. Okay.

KENT. So...

RAUL. So. Sounds like you just listed a bunch of reasons why he *should* do it.

KENT. Raul –

RAUL. No, I mean, you're talking about he needs to be fast, um, you know what helps people be fast? Strong leg muscles.

KENT. Yeah but –

RAUL. You know what helps people throw hard? Strong arms.

KENT. Okay but –

RAUL. And you're talking about he hits for average not for power and that just makes me think, like, okay, but what if he could do both?

KENT. I mean he needs to be nimble.

RAUL. See now you're just making words *up*.

KENT. He needs to stretch and bend and throw across his body to make plays! He's a fucking defensive player!

RAUL. *(overlapping)* No, I see.

KENT. *(overlapping)* And he doesn't have the frame in any case and you know it! You'll ruin his joints! You'll end his career!

RAUL. No, I get it, I see. Cause that would really fuck you up, huh? Cause you, you don't have to play defense, not really, just put your foot on the bag, stick out your arm, and hope that Adam, or Lance, or Terry, or whoever hits the bullseye, and that's good enough, and you're still a potential M.V.P. because you can park one every now and then. But –

KENT. Are *you* talking to *me* about defense? You can *barely* play right field, Raul.

RAUL. That's not –

KENT. Somebody goes the opposite way, you can feel the fans hoping you don't lose it in the sun or give up running before the warning track!

RAUL. That's not the point.

KENT. And don't talk to me about playing first base until you've tried to backhand a short hop from third coming in six feet up the foul line.

RAUL. That's not. My point. Kent.

KENT. What's your point.

RAUL. Cause, sure, you can hurt yourself if you do it *wrong*. But if you do it right? Why *not* him? How about a defensive dynamo who's also a slugger? Explosive from a standstill because his calves and thighs are huge. Tossing bullets from wherever the fuck he plays because his arms are jacked. And meanwhile he's hitting balls out, hitting for extra bases, average through the roof because he's getting walked because he's so fucking dangerous in the box, and then whenever he gets on he's a threat to steal, and everybody's just *quaking* at this guy. Why don't you want that for him? "Hey, Adam, sit down for the good of the team!" So concerned. *Fuck* you. That kid scares the *hell* out of you. And you're just worried that if *I* take him on? Suddenly *that's* what everybody's looking for. And that. Was my fucking. Point.

(There is a silence. **RAUL** *stands. And begins to walk off.)*

KENT. Where are you going?

RAUL. I'm going to get our pre-game vitamins.

KENT. Oh.

RAUL. Unless. Hm. Do you not want those now?

KENT. No. I mean yes. I do.

RAUL. So I can go get them?

KENT. Yes. But –

RAUL. What.

KENT. I mean, does it ever…?

RAUL. *What.*

KENT. *Bother* you?

RAUL. What? Why.

KENT. I don't know! Um. Ethically?

RAUL. *(beat)* What does that mean.

KENT. *Um.* That it's not exactly. I don't know. Fair? That it's. Kind of…

RAUL. What? That it's "kind of" what?

KENT. You know.

RAUL. No, I don't know, Kent, why don't you *tell* me.

KENT. I mean. Isn't it?

RAUL. Well let me answer your question with a question. Does it bother you that you're taller than most guys, so your reach is farther, and your stride is longer?

KENT. No.

RAUL. Does it bother you that you were born in a town that had some money so it had great baseball facilities?

KENT. No.

RAUL. Do you know where *I* was born?

KENT. I mean, not, no, not exactly –

RAUL. Because the way I see it? This is only way to *make* it fair. They are watching us *all the time,* guy. Is he hot? Is he slumping? We gonna hold onto him or cut him loose? For a few healthy years, Kent. And there's two ways it can go. Don't pan out and get traded like a chump? Or blow up like a superstar, go free agent and get paid.

This is not a team sport. Not anymore. You want to play with a handicap? You be my guest. But not me.

KENT. That's a great attitude, Raul.

RAUL. I know. I know it is.

KENT. This is not a team sport? Are you *nuts?* Who *cares* about putting up huge numbers if you're on a losing club, Raul? But also? You jackass? Free agency has some problems. Because the owners are colluding. "What does that mean?" It means they all get together and agree not to sign any free agents and nobody gets paid, so I don't care if you *are* a superstar, Raul, because, the fact is you need the union. Which is full of guys who may or may not share your personal views on what's fair. So also? Don't call them our "pre-game vitamins." I know in your mind that counts as being subtle? But it's not subtle. It's fucking stupid. And anybody who heard you would know exactly what you were talking about. And who *knows* what happens then. *(beat)* And I am *not* scared of that fucking *kid.*

(pause)

RAUL. Kent?

KENT. Yeah.

RAUL. I know you're smarter than I am. I know that. Don't think I don't. But I also think? That you're a little bit of a coward. And a little bit of a snake. And so you can say whatever the fuck you want about me. You go ahead and you say it. But I am not either of those things.

(RAUL exits. Silence. KENT is alone. He fumes for a moment. Then he does a violent set on the bench press. During this, ADAM enters. He watches for a while. KENT finishes.)

ADAM. Should you really do that without anybody spotting you?

KENT. Oh. Hey. Feeling better?

ADAM. Yeah, that just… What the fuck is wrong with me?

KENT. Hey. Same thing used to happen to me.

ADAM. When you came up?

KENT. Oh, well, no, I mean, not really since like, uh, high school, but –

ADAM. Well it doesn't happen to me.

KENT. You're a rookie. And this is Game One of the World Series. It's okay.

ADAM. No. I mean. It's not the game.

KENT. It's okay if it's the game, Adam.

ADAM. It's not the game. It's a girl.

KENT. *(beat)* What?

ADAM. It's, uh… You know what? Never mind.

KENT. *(Smiling.)* You're upset about a girl?

ADAM. Oh, okay, haha, fine, yes, it's hilarious –

KENT. No – !

ADAM. See? This is exactly the kind of bullshit I figured I'd get from Raul, so I didn't say anything, but I thought that maybe with you, but no, here it is anyway, so that's just –

KENT. *(overlapping)* No. No, no. Just. Hey! Just. That's really sweet.

ADAM. Oh yeah? It doesn't *feel* too sweet.

KENT. This is that girl you've been seeing?

ADAM. Yeah.

KENT. What happened, man?

ADAM. I don't…! Nothing. Just. She broke up with me.

KENT. Just now?

ADAM. Yeah. Like. Right after we closed out the A.L.C.S.

KENT. Man.

ADAM. Like. Right before I play in the World Series.

KENT. Yeah, no, it's not very considerate.

ADAM. And I don't know. Just. I felt…safe? Because like. Why would she break up with a guy who's about to play in the World Series? Like. Isn't it actually really cool to be dating a guy who's doing that? So like. You know. It wasn't really a moment at which I was feeling like that could even happen. And then. It did. And now I'm in really bad shape, like, I always, with this stuff, I go to this place where I'm, like, I'm all up in my head, like, if I try to go out with somebody else, instead I'm just thinking about what she would think about what I'm doing, or I wonder what *she's* doing, which is *worse*, so I'm in this cloud of, like, memories, or all like anxious about if I'm gonna hear about her, or run into her, and this is, yeah, you're right, a really really inconvenient time for that, so, fuck, I'm sorry, this is lame and irrelevant, and I am such a loser, I apologize –

KENT. *(overlapping)* No, hey, no no, not at all. I'm, hey, I'm glad you feel like you can talk to me about this stuff.

ADAM. I…! *(beat)* Really? *(beat)* But I mean what do *you* know? You've been with the same girl since college. You're married. You've got a kid.

KENT. That's true.

ADAM. Yeah. *(beat)* No, I mean, come on, tell me, what do you *know*? You've been with same girl since college, you're married, you've –

KENT. Oh! Oh, oh.

ADAM. Yeah.

KENT. Oh, uh. Huh. Well, okay, first of all, forget the athlete thing. Forget it. Because why would you want to be with someone where that was the most important thing to them? Because with anybody worthwhile? I don't get the impression that the things we think are important to them are the same things they think are important. And second of all…? *(beat)* No, that's it. That's all I got.

ADAM. Well, thanks, even just… Because I couldn't… I mean *you* know Raul.

KENT. Yes I do.

ADAM. On top of which? On top of his own way of dealing with people? It's like the guy's invincible with this stuff, he feels nothing, no matter what any girl ever does, he just bounces back, like, instantly, and then there's two more in line, for which he's always game.

KENT. He feels it. He just...handles it in his own way.

ADAM. Great. He'll probably date my ex. *(Beat. He feels unwell.)* Ohhh.

KENT. Hey, whoa –

ADAM. No, I'm cool. I'm cool. Do you want me to spot you?

KENT. Oh. Uh.

ADAM. What.

KENT. I just. I don't know if you're strong enough.

ADAM. Oh.

KENT. I just mean in your present condition.

ADAM. Oh. Yeah. No.

KENT. I just... Even just the outside chance of you dropping a barbell on my throat moments before Game One –

ADAM. No. You're right. I should... *(He looks off.)* There's press out there?

KENT. Um. A, yes, a handful of the most dedicated baseball writers figured they'd cover the World Series this year, yeah.

ADAM. No. I mean. They scare the hell out of me anyway. I don't want to go out there and, like, vomit. On them. On camera.

KENT. You won't.

ADAM. What are they gonna ask me?

KENT. What do they usually ask you?

ADAM. Nothing. They don't usually talk to me at all. Except, you know. To ask about you or Raul.

KENT. Oh.

ADAM. I'm not good at talking to them like you are.

KENT. I'm not good at talking to them. Tony makes me.

ADAM. Well you seem good at it.

KENT. All I've got is this one trick that I find helpful.

ADAM. Yeah? What's that.

KENT. Oh. Well. I mean. Um. I could tell you? But this is a very special technique that is not to be trifled with. Okay?

ADAM. Um. Okay.

KENT. Seriously. If I pass this along to you, you must pledge always to use your powers for good, instead of evil.

ADAM. Uh. Okay. Sure.

KENT. Okay. Ready? Here it is. Speak? In really complete sentences.

ADAM. *(beat)* What?

KENT. Speak in sentences that are much much more complete than necessary.

ADAM. I don't get it.

KENT. Okay. I played for Team U.S.A. in '84. *Right* here, actually, all the games were in this park, which, first of all, was a real head trip for a bunch of amateurs, but it was also the first time I really had to do any of that stuff, be on T.V., deal with media, any of that, on any kind of big scale, and this was, I don't know if you remember, but there was a *boycott*, like, because we didn't go to Moscow the time before, all the Soviet countries didn't come here, and President *Reagan's* there, and everyone's asking all these questions. And I'm shy. I'm a really shy person when it comes down to it. So that's also when I figured out this trick. Because, basically? Anything these guys ask you, you can usually answer it in a word, or like a few words, but you could *also*? Pad that simple answer out to three, four, five times longer. And they think you're just being thorough or complete or something good? But what you're really doing is you're using your answer as a way of taking the time you need. To get ready. For the next one. "Hey, Adam, how do you hope play?" "Uhh. I want to play well." No. "What I'd *really* like is I'd like to be able to contribute *and* to make a real contribution. Here on the ballclub." They know what you want to contribute to. You don't have to say ballclub. Say it anyway. "Because I want to be able to give something back to all the great fans who have made me feel so welcome since I came here to play and to all my great teammates because you know we've got a great team here." They do know. They are professional sportswriters who cover your team for a living. Say it anyway. "Because, hey, we've got such a great bunch of guys here, Ricky, and Dave, and Big Dave," see because they also like it when you refer casually to the other people on the team by their first names, like you're all really tight, for some reason they love that, "and Raul, and of course Kent, it's great to have Kent to look up to, to have a real star and a real hero in the clubhouse to model yourself on." And, by the way, if you listen to Raul talk to them, this is the exact opposite of what he does, but, fact is, *you're* the one who gets to set the pace. Because they don't get to ask the next question whenever they want. They can only ask it when you stop talking. And you do not stop talking until you're ready. And it's not so you have time to dwell on what you said before, and it's not because you're planning, you *can't*, cause you don't know what's coming. It's taking the time. Just to stay in that one question till you are done with it. You hold that fucking moment till it's over. *(pause)* Do you understand what I'm saying to you?

ADAM. Yeah. *(beat)* Right. You're right. We got this.

KENT. Yes. See? Yes.

ADAM. The Dodgers? Please.

KENT. You read the scouting report on these guys?

ADAM. Yeah. We got this.

KENT. A.L.C.S. Those guys were supposed to be so tough. What happened?

ADAM. We kicked ass.

KENT. So *these* clowns? Come on.

ADAM. No. You're right. We got them on offense. They're playing hurt. Gibson's out of the lineup so we don't have to worry about that guy.

KENT. But even on pitching! Please. We took out *Clemens.* We *got* these guys.

ADAM. And hey! What kind of a name is "Orel Hershiser"?

KENT. Oh. Um. I don't know. It's, like, Mormon, I think, or –?

ADAM. No, just, it's kind of a ridiculous…name I'm…
saying… *(beat)* Yeah. *(beat)* See, Kent, the thing about
you is…

KENT. What.

ADAM. I mean, a lot of guys with your ability? They, uh…
They're fucking pricks? But you, I mean, you've got
this… You don't feel like you have to be… You're, like.
A good player? *And* nice. Which is. It's cool. *(pause)* So,
wait, how'd you guys do?

KENT. What?

ADAM. At the Games.

KENT. Oh. Lost in the finals to Japan. So, silver. Or. Woulda
been.

ADAM. Right.

KENT. Hey. Do you want to try to do a set?

ADAM. What?

KENT. Just. Since you're here. Do you – ?

*(RAUL enters. He is carrying a small, black, medical
bag. A moment)*

RAUL. Hey. Adam. Listen, uh –

KENT. We're sort of in the middle of something, Raul.

RAUL. Well I have something important to discuss with
him.

KENT. Dude.

RAUL. What.

KENT. Well, I mean, just… I mean, if you…

RAUL. What.

(Pause. KENT can't say anything in front of ADAM.)

ADAM. What is it.

RAUL. I just wanted to tell you. That you got it.

ADAM. What? What. *(pause)* Who says.

RAUL. Tony.

ADAM. Tony said that?

RAUL. Well, like you said, they're not gonna announce till after the series, after the season, but the sense he's got, from talking to the people who vote? Is it's you. You got it. Rookie of the fucking Year.

ADAM. But, I mean, he's just saying, like, the general sense he got.

RAUL. I heard the same way. Kent too.

ADAM. Huh.

RAUL. Back to back to back, baby! Wooooo!

ADAM. Wow. I mean. Wow.

KENT. That's great, Adam. That's really great. *(to RAUL)* Anything else?

RAUL. No. That's it.

KENT. Okay.

RAUL. Okay. *(pause)* After you.

ADAM. What are you guys doing?

RAUL. Grown-up stuff. You wouldn't understand.

ADAM. What?

KENT. He's joking. It's just. Our pre-game...thing. It's a ritual. A ritual thing. Uh. *(beat)* Congratulations, Adam. Seriously. I...

(A moment. KENT goes. RAUL turns back to ADAM.)

RAUL. Hey. *(pause)* Think how stupid. That fucking bitch. Is gonna feel now.

(beat)

ADAM. What? *(beat)* You, uh... How did you...?

(RAUL goes. ADAM is alone. A silence. ADAM smiles.)

ADAM. Man. *(pause)* Oh man. *(pause)* That feels good.

3.
April 1994
Texas

(A locker room. RAUL is at his locker. He is now wearing a different team's uniform. He is talking to the press. During the following, he undresses and by the end of the speech he is wearing only a towel.)

RAUL. It doesn't look good. It does not look good. Because why? Because the atmosphere is poisoned already by behaviors on the part of ownership that have created a lot of mistrust even going into the thing. Which, it's complicated, so I don't expect everybody here to have total familiarity, but, there was a problem with free agency where the owners were doing something called "colluding", that prevented a lot of guys from getting paid, somehow, and, honestly, somebody shoulda done something sooner, somebody on the inside who could just be honest and break it open, instead of everybody looking the other way because they want to get their piece, or, if there's some code of silence amongst the owners, then, I don't know, somebody else shoulda been in there, the government, somebody should have had someone in there, you know, wearing a wire, like they do. Don't they do that? Like, the F.B.I.? Whatever. Cause instead we got robbed. And so the way we're even going in, I mean, when people feel they've been treated that way, you know, cheated, they're that much more likely just to get up and walk. So this is not the time for them to come at us talking about a salary cap, or trying to sneak up on that all subtle by attaching it to revenue sharing. And, whatever, I'm not one of those guys who's gonna tell you that they're a bunch of assholes either, excuse me, but, I mean, take my owner, he's a good guy, a personable guy, so there are some good guys on the other side of the table, and maybe they'll come at us with respect. But if they just try to bulldoze cause they think we're not gonna *strike*, well, they're in for a surprise. Not that I'm *hoping* for it. I hope it doesn't happen. Because, just for me, personally, I'm really starting to find my groove here in Texas, you know? Cause I was never totally comfortable out West, never really got along too well with Tony, never felt totally appreciated, cause, like, no matter what I did, it was always more about some bullshit, or just some irrelevancy, excuse me, that was going on off the field, so I was actually even a little relieved when they traded me. So I've got a really good feeling about this year. I've got some great new kids to play with, Ivan and Raffy, to mentor, or whatnot. And it feels like, finally, it could be my time. To be known. For what I really am. Hold on a second. *(He yells off to one side.)* Do we seriously have to have the lady reporters in the locker room? I'm in a towel here.

4.
May 1995
New England

(Another locker room. RAUL is at his locker. He is in a towel. He is talking to the press. During the following, he changes into yet another different team's uniform and by the end of the speech he is fully dressed.)

RAUL. I mean, it's complicated. But what I wish? Is I really wish more of the top guys had been able to see, you know, the link, between a salary cap and revenue sharing, by which I mean the practice of *sharing revenue,* which, combined with a *cap* on *salaries,* could have prevented this whole thing. But instead, we cut off the whole season and everybody in the whole country's feelings about the entire game of baseball are jeopardized because of just the greed that everybody exhibited through the whole thing. But you know what, guys? I think? A great player? Who is playing great? Could really help the game to bounce back from all this. But, see instead, with you guys, it's, you know, it's Bad Boy Raul is in town, and what kind of trouble is he gonna get into on the club, and what kind of shenanigans is he going to be involved in, and once again that's the story, and, frankly, I mean, I just, I find it kinda interesting, why a guy like me, or Barry, is the bad guy all the time, while another guy might not be the focus, and why *that* might be, instead of, oh, let's knock Raul again, because had some stupid injuries he could have avoided, or got hit on the head by a fly ball one time, or was maybe caught five years ago for speeding, or, whatever, crashing, because he was worked up from a fight he had with his wife at the time that, okay, maybe it got a little physical, but which was the whole reason he was speeding in the first place, and we've been divorced four years now, so leave it alone already, or who had a handgun *one time* in his car that the cops only even *found* because he left it on the seat after he accidentally, okay, *accidentally* parked in the handicapped spot at a hospital, which was the only reason they even looked, like it's not like I was even *holding* it! Because if that's the kind of thing that you guys want to write about, again, this year, instead of something positive? Then you guys go ahead and write about that. And I'll just know? In my heart? That that tells me a hell of a lot more about you guys than it says anything at all about me. Now if you'll excuse me I have a game to play.

5.
April 1997
Northern California

(A Manager's Office. **KENT** *is wearing nice street clothes and the team cap of his original team. He is talking on the phone.)*

KENT. It's not what you think...it, it just, it's not what you think...I understand...I understand that...I understand that, believe me, I see why you think that, I see why it looks that way from your perspective, but...well, okay...not, I'm not, look, I'm not denying anything, how can...because I don't even know what you're...I... Of course...Of course I do...Of course I love you... yes...I love you too...I do...that has nothing to, and, and, it's not, in any case, it's not even – !

(The door opens. **RAUL** *enters. He is back in the workout clothes of his original team.* **KENT** *makes a "come on in" gesture but then holds up a "just a minute" finger.* **RAUL** *nods and looks around.* **KENT** *continues to talk on the phone.)*

KENT. *(on the phone)* Listen, I can't continue this right now...I know...I know...I, look, someone just came in, and I need to deal with it, and I cannot continue to have this conversation right now...okay...yes...I will...I will...I, listen, I said that I will...okay...I...Hello?... Hello?...

*(***KENT*** hangs up the phone. A moment. Looks up.)*

KENT. Hey!

RAUL. Hey.

KENT. Welcome back!

RAUL. Thanks. Thank you, man.

KENT. How are you doing?

RAUL. Fine. How are *you* doing?

KENT. Oh, uh. Fine. Good. Just. Fine. Feel good to be back?

RAUL. Uh. Sure. Yeah.

KENT. You get to meet everybody?

RAUL. What?

KENT. The new kids. Miguel, Jason –

RAUL. Oh. Uh. Yeah. They seem like good kids.

KENT. Yeah. They are. They are. *(beat)* What did you think when you got the call? Could you believe it?

RAUL. I don't know. I just figured Tony took whatever personal grudge he had with him when he left and the new guy just wants to win.

KENT. Oh is that right?

RAUL. Well, let's see, how many championships since I left, it was, what was it... *(He pretends to count to a very high number on his fingers.)* Zero.

KENT. Yeah.

RAUL. How is the new skip?

KENT. Oh, good. He's good. *(beat)* I mean, it's a little...

RAUL. What.

KENT. No, nothing.

RAUL. He obviously likes you.

KENT. What?

RAUL. He let's you use his office.

KENT. Oh –

RAUL. What the hell are you doing in here?

KENT. Oh. Just. Privacy.

RAUL. For phone calls.

KENT. For instance.

RAUL. I do not have good memories of this room.

KENT. No?

RAUL. No. I was only ever in here for Tony to yell. Or, you know, trade me.

KENT. Well let's put an end to that. I mean, hey, if you're lucky, this is where you end up, right?

RAUL. What?

KENT. You know, managing. Or upstairs even, front office, instead of, whatever. Broke. Or in the hospital. *(pause)* Close the door.

(A moment. **RAUL** *closes the door.)*

RAUL. Uh. "You cutting me from the team already coach?"

KENT. Heh. Yeah right.

RAUL. Right? The "close the door" conversation –

KENT. Yeah, no, uh, "This isn't easy for me to say, kid. You've been a great asset to the team. But – "

RAUL. "Oh come on, coach, just gimme another chance!"

KENT. "You had plenty of chances. Plenty!"

*(***RAUL*** *chuckles.* **KENT** *joins in. They chuckle for a moment. Then, silence.)*

RAUL. Uh. What's up?

KENT. What did you notice about the new guys?

RAUL. What do you mean?

KENT. Anything that...caught your eye.

RAUL. Caught my eye? Uh. I don't think so.

KENT. You don't think so?

RAUL. Why do you ask?

KENT You tell me.

RAUL. *(loudly)* I don't even know what the fuck we're talking about, Kent.

KENT. You don't?

RAUL. No.

(A moment. **KENT** *lifts his shirt.* **RAUL** *looks him over and pats him down a little.)*

KENT. Okay?

RAUL. Just, you know –

KENT. Yeah, I do know, I know that you think you live in a movie. Okay?

RAUL. Okay. *(pause)* All right. So what have you been doing to those kids?

KENT. What am I *doing* to them?

RAUL. Yeah, because, and I assume this is what you're getting at, because, for example, Jason? Looks like he's filled with water.

KENT. Okay –

RAUL. So, yeah, man, what are you *doing* to them?

KENT. Okay, first of all, I haven't been doing anything *to* them. Second of all, whatever it is that's been *happening*, it's been according to a very specific regimen that is not something that I myself pioneered or developed.

RAUL. Oh, I see, so it's *my* fault.

KENT. It's your system.

RAUL. Whoa, okay –

KENT. No, I'm just, I'm saying now that you're *back* –

RAUL. *(overlapping)* No, hold on, because, if somebody, hell *yes*, it's mine, no *doubt*, but if a certain someone who doesn't really know exactly what he's doing is the one that's passing it along, without direct supervision, then that person is the one that is fucking it up.

KENT. I am not fucking anything up.

RAUL. Oh? Huh. See, because, after I left here? Didn't you spend, like, the next *two seasons* hurt?

KENT. What?

RAUL. Once I was no longer watching over you, Kent. In '93. You barely played cause you were hurt. And '94.

KENT. There was a strike in '94.

RAUL. There was a strike and you were hurt.

KENT. I hurt my *foot*, it wasn't... What's your *point*?

RAUL. Just –

KENT. And weren't *you* hurt *all the time*? In Texas?

RAUL. Hey, okay –

KENT. *And* back East? *And* here? Aren't you just like a nonstop festival of time on the D.L.?

RAUL. That has nothing to do with anything. I've been that way since I was a kid.

KENT. Oh, so some injuries have to do with something, and some don't have to do with anything, and you're the expert on which is which?

RAUL. You don't have to... *(beat)* Look, I just want to hear you say it.

KENT. What. Say what.

RAUL. The words, the specific words, I want to hear you say the words.

KENT. What are you talking about?

RAUL. Here. I'll help you get started. "Raul, I need you… to…"

KENT. What.

RAUL. Say it. Out loud. Specifically. "Raul, I need you to…"

(*A moment.* KENT *looks at* RAUL *curiously. Then suspiciously. Then he grabs* RAUL*'s shirt and tears it open, looks around on his chest, pats him down, during which:*)

RAUL. Hey! What the fuck, man, the fuck are you doing – ?

KENT. *(overlapping)* Just, let me, just let me, come on –

RAUL. *(overlapping)* Who the fuck is being paranoid is now? Jesus.

(KENT. *backs off. A moment.*)

KENT. Sorry.

RAUL. Yeah. *(A moment.)*

KENT. I just –

RAUL. *What.*

KENT. I don't know! Just –

RAUL. There's a code, bitch. What do you think I am? There's a fucking code.

KENT. Oh but you thought *I* was wired.

RAUL. Yeah. I did.

KENT. I see. Cool. *(beat)* Okay so then what were you trying to get me to say?

RAUL. What do you think, man? That you need me. Because I know best. Because I'm the king. *(beat)* Dude, if I wanted to dime you out, I wouldn't be all stupid and blatant about it, come on! I'd sneak up on it

KENT. I, uh –

RAUL. I'd be subtle as a motherfucker.

KENT. I'm sure you would.

(*pause*)

RAUL. So?

KENT. So? What. *(pause)* Seriously? *(pause)* Um. Okay. Raul?

RAUL. Yeah.

KENT. I need you. Because you know best. Because you're the king.

(beat)

RAUL. See now I don't know —

KENT. Jesus Christ —

RAUL. No, because, I mean, doesn't it *bother* you? Isn't it a little, uh — ?

KENT. *(overlapping)* Oh I see. Okay. Yes. Haha. It's hilarious.

RAUL. *(overlapping)* What was that? I couldn't hear you from up here on my high horse.

KENT. See I thought maybe we could just, but no, here we go —

RAUL. Well, come on, I mean, when I left, you were kind of on the fence about it. Now you're Johnny Appleseed? What gives?

KENT. I don't know! *(beat)* Jason hits a ton. We haven't had a prospect in the infield like Miguel since we traded Adam in '92, *before* that, really, since Adam wasn't even Adam anymore by '92. We've got some pitching. I don't know. This club could go all the way.

(beat)

RAUL. Well, but it's even tougher now, you know that, right?

KENT. What do you mean? Testing's a joke, which, if that isn't the tacit approval of management I don't know *what* is, so —

RAUL. No I mean but *now* it's even against the *law*.

KENT. Oh, why, because Congress *said* so, like a half a second ago? That's politics, man. *We're* the ones who actually have to go *out* there every day, while they sit up there in Washington, and it's all over the league now, *pitchers* even, so I'm gonna send my boys, fucking *defenseless*, into *that?* No, sir. *(pause)* *What*, Raul, *what*, what *is* it?

(beat)

RAUL. "Since Adam wasn't even Adam anymore by '92."

KENT. What.

RAUL. What does that *mean?*

KENT. I don't know, just –

RAUL. You had a pretty shitty year yourself in '91 if you remember.

KENT. Okay.

RAUL. You hit .201. The only reason you didn't drop below the Mendoza Line is Tony sat you down the last game. To protect your *average*. To *protect* you.

KENT. Yes. I remember. So?

RAUL. So a lot of different factors go into trades.

KENT. Well you ought to know.

RAUL. Heh. Zing. Okay. But, what I mean is, *anybody* can slump, but *certain* guys get another chance, and then another chance, and so I just find it kind of interesting to hear you, of all people, knocking Adam like that, when maybe, if *somebody* had protected him they had the chance, we wouldn't need Miguel *or* Jason, or whoever else, filling up his spot.

KENT. Adam is doing fine –

RAUL. Oh *now* he's *fine* –

KENT. He is a major league baseball player.

RAUL. Yeah? Where.

KENT. I don't know. *Some*where. What do you – ?

RAUL. *(overlapping)* Somewhere?

KENT. What, now it's my job to keep *tabs?* He's not my *responsibility.*

RAUL. Oh now he's *not* your responsibility.

KENT. Adam got *married,* he had a *kid* –

RAUL. *(overlapping)* The, *what?* The fuck does *that* have to do with anything?

(beat)

KENT. I don't know what you want me to say. Are you gonna help me out or not.

(The phone on the desk rings. It rings a second time.
RAUL *gestures to the phone.* **KENT** *picks up the receiver*
and hangs it up immediately. A moment.)

RAUL. You want me running this, I'll run it, but you gotta
follow my lead. I mean I see how it is. You've been
here nine years, Tony's gone, new guy's nice enough
to let you kick him out of his office, but I don't want
any prima donna crap. Not only are we're gonna cor-
rect whatever you're doing, but I've picked up a thing
or two. In my years. In the wilderness. We're gonna
take this to a whole nother level. Okay?

KENT. Okay.

*(***RAUL*** *turns to go. Then hesitates.)*

RAUL. Did you *ask* for me?

KENT. What?

RAUL. Did you tell the new skip. To go for me.

KENT. I'm not management, Raul. I just go out and play.

(A moment. Then **RAUL** *opens the door.)*

RAUL. You want to work out? I'm going to do a back routine.

KENT. I did back already today.

RAUL. Want to do it again?

KENT. I already did three.

RAUL. Wanna spot me?

KENT. You don't need a spotter to do back.

RAUL. Hey. Uhhh. Okay.

(A moment. **RAUL** *goes. Leaves the door open.* **KENT** *goes*
to the door. Closes it. Goes back to the phone. Picks up
the phone.)

6.
July 1997
The Midwest

(A general manager's office. **KENT** *is wearing nice street clothes. He is talking to the press. During the following, he puts on the cap, and perhaps also holds up the jersey, of a different team.)*

KENT. Geez. Well. I'm not really thinking about it is the truth. And I honestly don't know how to account for it. I mean, first of all everybody's saying that there's different balls now, that the league's using these new ones which are more juiced, and, I don't know, it does seem like guys are getting a little more pop. And people are saying it maybe has to do with the expansion clubs, diluting the talent, on top of which the umps are calling a smaller zone, they've been tightening up the zone, harder to hit the corners. And also the league's building all these new parks, you know, these nostalgia, throwback parks, and the dimensions are different, a little smaller, and for me personally, it's, you know, it's, I've been around longer, you get better at reading pitchers, psyching guys out, getting ahead in the count, you refine your swing, everything. So, I don't know, you know, it's all of that, mixed together, and who's to say what the key factor is. All I know is I'm having a good year, hitting real well, hitting a lot of balls out, the fans are real excited again, and the hope now is that switching teams won't have any kind of a negative impact on my performance. But then I'm playing for Tony again, so, and, you know, it was always a little weird for me out West after he left. So if anything I think it might help me. To, you know, to go ahead do the job I came here to do and make the contribution I'm expected to make for all my great teammates and the great fans who've made me feel so welcome. Here on the ballclub. Otherwise, other than that, I'm just not giving the subject a whole lot of thought.

7.
July 1998
Colorado

(A dugout. KENT is looking out at the field. He is wearing a National League All-Star uniform and the cap from the previous scene.)

KENT. Okay. Come on now. Swing away. Let's see what you got. *(A moment. He applauds.)* That's it. That's what I'm talking about. Yeah. Now. One more. One more just like that. Come on. *(A moment. He applauds again.)* There it is. There it is. Yeah.

(ADAM has walked up behind KENT. He also wears a National League All-Star uniform and the cap of his new team.)

ADAM. "You hold that moment till it's over."

(KENT turns.)

KENT. What's up, rook!

ADAM. Hey man!

(ADAM goes for the handshake. KENT goes for the hug. They hug awkwardly.)

KENT. *Gosh* it's good to see you.

ADAM. I know, right? Too long, too long. Look at *you*, man! Damn!

KENT. What.

ADAM. You're friggin huge, man! "Superman" indeed.

KENT. Oh, god, yeah. I was fine with "Kent"? But I guess journalists get bored easy. *(The cap.)* That's right! You're down South now!

ADAM. Yeah.

KENT. You like it there?

ADAM. *(Shrugs.)* Great team.

KENT. Yeah, man. Great club. *Great* pitching.

ADAM. Our rotation is indeed fierce.

KENT. Seriously, every time you face those guys, you're

happy it's not one guy, turns out it's another guy, Glavine, Maddux, Smoltz –

ADAM. Some of them are here.

KENT. What?

ADAM. Greg and Tommy, they're here. You want to meet them?

KENT. I, uh… *(beat)* I've met them, Adam. I've been in this thing before.

ADAM. Oh, yeah, no. Right. That's right.

KENT. Yeah. *(beat)* That's right! This is your first All-Star Game!

ADAM. Yeah.

KENT. Congratulations, Adam. That is really awesome.

ADAM. Yeah, no, thanks, yeah. He comes up, he breaks in, and ten short years later he makes the National League All-Star Team. It's a really overwhelming story.

KENT. Hey, knock that crap off. You're an All-Star second baseman.

ADAM. Actually they play me in center.

KENT. I, really? *(beat)* Point is I never doubted it would happen for you.

ADAM. You don't have to say that.

KENT. Don't listen to me. You're the one got the votes.

ADAM. I, um, I didn't actually, no.

KENT. What?

ADAM. My manager's the National League Team manager, so –

KENT. Right.

ADAM. So he just put me on the team.

KENT. Right, yeah, no, right. *(beat)* But! The support of your manager. Who sees you play every day. Over the opinion of some fans who may or may not be even watching, I mean, *that's* –

ADAM. No. Yes. It's nice to have a manager who believes in me.

KENT. Ahh, fuck Tony. You ever look at his stats from when he played?

ADAM. Well, okay, but managing is a different skill, and that one he's got, I mean, he'll get into the Hall of Fame for managing, so that's not exactly –

KENT. Well, no, I mean, you're right, you're probably right. I'm just saying. *(beat)* Or, hey, then maybe look at it that way.

ADAM. What? What.

KENT. That there's a way to have a whole second career. If it doesn't pan out for a guy. As a player.

ADAM. Oh.

KENT. But, no, I mean, hey, don't sell yourself short. Here you are.

ADAM. Here I am. *(Beat. Then, pointing.)* You taking batting practice?

KENT. Did already. Just sticking around to watch. You?

ADAM. Yeah. I'm…coming up.

(A moment.)

KENT. Okay. Bring it on home now. Come on. Bring it on home.

ADAM. *(simultaneously)* Swing away. Show it to me. Show me what you got.

(A moment. They applaud together.)

KENT. That's what I'm talking about. Nice. Now keep it up.

ADAM. *(simultaneously)* Righteous. Cannot argue with that. One more like it.

(A moment.)

ADAM. Yeah I always sort of badmouthed it? Meaningless game, empty spectacle, Home Run Derby, souvenir t-shirts. But I gotta say actually being here? Pretty much kicks ass. Especially after such a rough year.

KENT. Right. *(beat)* Oh! Hey. My god. Yes. How's your wife?

ADAM. Oh, thanks, she's fine. Thank you. She's doing good.

KENT. Great.

ADAM. She's here actually. She's here to watch the game.

KENT. So she's all recovered.

ADAM. Oh, well, I mean, recovery means different things? The issue now is what impact the whole thing had on her immune system. Like if it's gonna be easier for her to get sick in the future? But, yes, we're okay now as far as the initial scare is concerned, yeah.

KENT. Well you guys seemed to handle it well. I mean, from what I read and saw.

ADAM. Yeah, suddenly the press wanted to talk to me again.

KENT. No, just, I mean –

ADAM. No, yeah, you're right, we hung in there. I mean, we also totally collapsed. Like, after it was over? I don't know. Something like that you sort of put your feelings aside for the duration. But then as soon as there was time we both just lost it. *(pause)* At least out here you know when you're up, right? Out there nobody tells you when those moments are gonna be.

KENT. Well. It's really good that you guys have each other.

ADAM. Definitely. Definitely. *(beat)* Oh, god, Kent, yeah. I was really sorry to hear that you split up.

KENT. Oh yeah. Thanks.

ADAM. No, I always liked you guys together.

KENT. Uh, me too.

ADAM. I mean. You don't have to talk about it. I'm just saying I'm sorry.

KENT. Yeah, no, thanks. It's okay. *(beat)* I mean, whatever, I had some… I wasn't totally… *(beat)* I'm a professional athlete. It can be hard for us to stick those out. You know?

ADAM. Can be.

(A moment.)

KENT. Okay! Park this one. Just park it. All the way.

ADAM. *(simultaneously)* Okay now swing down, make sure you're down on it.

(A moment. They applaud together.)

KENT. What did I tell you. What. Did. I. Tell. You.

ADAM. *(simultaneously)* If not now when. If not now then tell me when.

(A moment.)

KENT. So! Any tips?

ADAM. What?

KENT. About this park. You played here for a while, right?

ADAM. Oh, no, yeah, I was here. After Florida.

KENT. That's right. You hit *all* the expansion clubs.

ADAM. Uh. Yeah.

KENT. So?

ADAM. You'll do fine. New park. Hitter friendly. Also something about the Colorado altitude. Thin. Air. Something. *(beat)* Whatever, who am I talking to? The year you're having. *(beat)* I mean, you're on pace, Kent. You're on *the* pace.

KENT. That's what they tell me. I'm not really thinking about it.

ADAM. Well, you've got, what, thirty-five, *now*, thirty-six, at the break? So –

KENT. Thirty-seven.

ADAM. Thirty-seven home runs at the break? You've never put up numbers like this. Not this fast.

KENT. If you say so. Like I said I'm not really –

ADAM. Sure. No. Sure. *(beat)* But, I mean, come *on*.

KENT. Hey. One game at a time. One at bat at a time. Anything else, you've gotta just get control of it in your mind, and put a cap on it, otherwise –

ADAM. Okay. But. I mean, come *on*. It's me, Kent. It's Adam.

KENT. So…?

ADAM. So talk to me for real.

KENT. Hey, give me a break, okay? We're only halfway through the season, so don't talk to me like it's definitely gonna happen, because then I'm gonna feel extra stupid when it doesn't. It could easily not.

ADAM. No. I know.

KENT. So okay.

ADAM. That's not what I'm saying.

KENT. Well good. *(beat)* Wait, what are you saying?

ADAM. Just. What do you think it is?

KENT. What do I think what is.

ADAM. Come on. This is me.

KENT. Yeah. You said that already.

ADAM. So what do you think is going on?

KENT. Okay. Well. First of all. It's happening all over the league.

ADAM. What's happening.

KENT. Uh. The numbers, the huge numbers getting put up.

ADAM. Well, okay, but so then –

KENT. And? It's not like this is some sudden jump for me either. I hit fifty-eight last year.

ADAM. Yes. You were also pretty exceptional last season. Oh, hey, you know who else is having a pretty good year.

KENT. Who.

ADAM. Raul.

KENT. Is he?

ADAM. Up in Toronto.

KENT. That where he is now?

ADAM. Yeah. He's charging back this year. Really on a tear.

KENT. Good for him.

ADAM. Man. I haven't seen that guy in a long time. How's he doing?

KENT. Your guess is as good as mine.

ADAM. Oh. Uh. Okay. *(beat)* Okay! No pitcher. No pitcher. Drill this one. *(A moment. He does an announcer voice and applauds. Alone.)* "He got all of that one…long fly ball to deep left field…he's gonna run out of room…to the wall…! Gone!"

(A moment.)

KENT. Is there something you're trying to ask me, Adam?

ADAM. What? What.

KENT. Because if there's something you want to ask me then I wish that you would go ahead and just fucking ask me instead of roping me into what I thought was going to be like a pleasant conversation about catching up with and old friend that at this point I am no longer enjoying at all.

(beat)

ADAM. Well, okay, Kent. I mean, I'm not real slow. When we played together, I knew what was going on. I knew. And we were just coming up, and we were young, we were kids, Jesus, I look at these rooks now... And also I can't say what happened after I left. Of course not. All I know are the stats. But what I'd like to think? Is that you stopped. That maybe you felt bad about it, mentally, and that's why you started to struggle. And that maybe you tried to push yourself too hard without them and so that's how you hurt your foot. Maybe that's not what happened but that is what I'd like to think. But this? Nothing explains this. And so I guess what I'm asking is for you to tell me to my face. Cause I'm not a reporter. I'm not Tony. I'm not the fans and I'm not your son. This is just me here. This is just Adam. Asking why you cheated, Kent. Why are you still cheating?

(A silence. ADAM waits. Then can't anymore.)

ADAM. Um...

KENT. *(He points.)* Shh, hey, hold on. Barry's coming up to take his cuts.

ADAM. Oh. Hey.

(They watch. A silence.)

KENT. I love that little batting practice net that the batting practice pitcher has to stand behind? I love that thing. It's pure fear. It's like. "Please don't hurt me Mr. Awesome Batter. Please don't strike me down with your mighty power." I love that. Look how this guy is throwing. It's like he thinks Barry's gonna kill him. *(beat)* You talk to that guy yet today?

ADAM. Who, Barry?

KENT. Oh my god. What a prick, right?

ADAM. Oh. Yeah. I guess.

KENT. What a total prick.

ADAM. Yeah. No. He is. *(beat)* Although. I mean. You know.

KENT. What.

ADAM. Just. It's possible that he maybe had to face some things that you and me didn't have to face.

KENT. Like what. What things. *(beat)* Oh.

(A moment. They watch. They react.)

KENT. Damn.

ADAM. Yeah. That is a sweet swing.

KENT. You're not kidding.

(A moment.)

KENT. So okay. Do you remember 1919?

ADAM. What?

KENT. Just –

ADAM. No, Kent, I do not remember 1919, as I was not exactly around.

KENT. Do you remember what *happened*.

ADAM. I think so. Yeah.

KENT. Black Sox. A handful of gangsters bribes the best team in the game to throw the World Series. So there everybody is. After the biggest thing in American sports just got *bought*. And the game is dead. Except. The thing back then that almost nobody could do? Was hit one out. Guys were parking fifteen a year, twenty, tops. And *that* made you a slugger. Not even. Those were flukes. You hit a fly ball and it happens to catch the wind and carry. Nobody's thinking about clearing the wall. It almost never happens. But then who comes along?

ADAM. *(beat)* So okay you're just not gonna –

KENT. Who comes along, Adam?

ADAM. Babe Ruth.

KENT. Until 1919 he's a pitcher, basically. Most homers he's ever hit in a season is 29. Second most is 11. After 1919, he gets traded to the Yankees, and instead of putting him in the rotation, which would be wise since the guy is a great pitcher, they put him in the outfield so he can focus on hitting. In 1920, he hits 54 home runs. In 1921? He hits 59. Nobody had ever done anything close to that. Black Sox broke everybody's heart and people thought it was going to take the game years to recover from that. A decade. If ever. Two seasons later all anybody's talking about is Babe Ruth. Who by the way? Was no angel. And when he hits 60 in 1927 everybody knows *that's* the best team ever. Fuck the Black Sox. It's Murderer's Row. Gehrig, Combs, Dugan. Ruth.

ADAM. Okay, but –

> (**KENT** *puts a hand on* **ADAM**'s *shoulder, silencing him. A moment.* **KENT** *looks at* **ADAM** *earnestly as though he's going to say something else. Then, instead, slides his other hand up* **ADAM**'s *shirt.* **ADAM** *allows it, not resisting.* **KENT** *brings his hand back out after a moment. Clutching a wire and a tiny microphone, a length of duct tape still dangling from it. A moment. Then,* **KENT** *brings the microphone deliberately near his mouth and speaks directly into it.)*

KENT. And, yeah, I got shook up a little, with pressure to perform, and I had some injuries, because this game is hard, but I came back from that, and that is one of the things I've done I'm *proudest* of, and, yeah, *you* weren't there, because *you* got traded, because *you* weren't living up to your potential, because *you cracked* like a *little bitch*, even though a guy like you doesn't have *half* of what I do resting on his shoulders for the survival of the fucking sport, and now you're gonna get in my face with this melodramatic and accusatory horseshit like you can talk from some place of moral superiority when all you really did was fail? *Fuck* you. Now is there anything else? Because if not I think we're done.

*(**KENT** drops the microphone and turns back out. A moment. **KENT** claps.)*

KENT. Okay. That's right. We've got a team here. We have got a team.

*(During this, **ADAM** tears the microphone the rest of the way off, and shoves it into his pocket. A long silence. When at last they do speak it is without looking at each other.)*

ADAM. Well that is a great attitude, Kent.

KENT. *What?*

ADAM. The Black Sox threw the series because their owners treated them like slaves. We went on strike because *our* owners had a *labor dispute* with our *union*. It's not the same. Babe Ruth? Sure, he, lived on whiskey and cigars and he was really fat and he had a ton of women and he was kind of a cocky bastard, but he *played* straight, Kent. He played it straight. Man, those guys played the *game.* Work the count, draw the walk, steal second, take third on the hit and run, score on the sac fly, the actual *game* –

KENT. *This* is the game, Adam. *I'm* playing the game.

ADAM. Yeah everybody's on board. Ownership on down. Why not? The fans are back. So, hey, forget leveling the field, let's all watch rich teams from big cities beat up poor teams from small cities with nothing but home runs. So I don't care if you are the savior of the sport, Kent, because the fact is the sport is fucked. *(pause)* So you know what I think? I think it *should* have been years. A decade. If ever. I think when something like that happens? It's supposed to hurt. Real bad. For a long long time. I think that's how you learn enough so that next time? You approach the thing with a little bit more fucking respect.

(pause)

KENT. So, what, you got caught?

ADAM. I… What? Caught at what.

KENT. I mean they caught you and flipped you, right? You cut a deal?

ADAM. This isn't a movie, Kent. And I never did anything to get caught *at.*

KENT. Okay. So, then, what do you want. A fucking medal?

(*pause*)

ADAM. I'm up.

(**ADAM** *starts up the steps.*)

KENT Rook.

(*A moment.* **ADAM** *goes.* **KENT** *remains, alone. A moment. Then,* **KENT** *applauds.*)

KENT That's it, rook. Keep your head down. (*Pause. Then he applauds again.*) Nice. Don't force it. (*Pause. He applauds.*) There it is. On the screws. (*Pause. Then, to himself.*) On the screws.

8.
February 2005
|Colorado

(A batting cage. ADAM is by a pitcher's mound. He is now wearing yet another different team's cap and starter jacket. He is talking to the press.)

ADAM. Well, first of all, no. I haven't read it. I have not. I mean, from my understanding, it hasn't even been published, right? But, um, the way it's been described to me is, basically, he talks about his experiences, and things he did, and also things he says all kinds of other guys all did, and goes so far, is my understanding, as to, like, advocate this stuff? To say this a good thing, and everybody should try this, and do this, and if you're an athlete and you don't do this, you're just being stupid, which... *(pause)* I'd hope he would find better things to do with his time, better ways to contribute, and to make a contribution, than by writing a book where he's using the names of all these guys, Sammy, and Jason, and Ivan, and Barry, and Miguel, and Raffy... and Kent...to advocate something like that. *(pause)* Because, on top of which, on top of just the unsavoryness, to my mind, of the whole enterprise, is the fact that it's not even true. I mean, this is a long time ago now, but I never witnessed anything, nothing, that would indicate that that was the case. I mean, weights weren't even a part of the game back then. Most guys in the game wouldn't even lift. And it's not hard to imagine various motivations Raul might have for writing those things now, like, if he's just mad, with how his own career turned out, and the kind of attention he got, as opposed to Kent, and all the attention that he got, and feeling excluded from that, you know, them having come up together, well... *(beat)* But, look, I mean, obviously, it's not even particularly or really relevant to me, which is I guess one small thing to be grateful for, or at least my understanding is, is that I myself am not mentioned in it at all. Or, like, barely mentioned. In one sentence. Like, literally, that my name comes up once, and he doesn't seem to have any idea what position I even played, and he basically just sort of acknowledges he knew me. And that I was there.

9.
March 2005
Washington, DC

(A side room in the United States Capitol. RAUL is here, wearing a suit. A long silence. RAUL takes out a bottle of pills. Takes a pill. KENT enters. He is also wearing a suit. And glasses. A moment.)

RAUL. Oh! Oh. Hey.

KENT. Hi.

RAUL. Uh. Hey.

KENT. Hey.

(RAUL puts the bottle of pills and the bottle of water away.)

RAUL. Um. This, uh, they told me, uh… *(pause)* I'm supposed to, I'm just, you know, waiting. In this room. Until, uh…

(A silence. KENT just stares at RAUL.)

RAUL. How is everybody? Is everybody here? Are they nervous? I'm nervous. A little shaky, a… Just, talking in public, you know? And I hear they got all these weird little rituals and things you're supposed to follow? So, that was just, I was just, to calm me *down,* just taking some…

(A silence. RAUL waits for KENT to speak. KENT just stares.)

RAUL. You found me, okay? They hid me and you found me. Good job. I guess they just figured it would be better for everybody if I was separate from, you know, until we were actually *in* the thing. But if you, I mean, there's not, I don't have a, just, okay, look, Kent, I wrote a book, okay? I wrote a book. Just to talk about my life and some of my thoughts and feelings and beliefs and things that happened to me which I have the right to talk about because they *happened* to me, okay?

KENT. Okay.

RAUL. And I definitely didn't know that there would be congressional fucking *hearings*. Okay? I never paid attention to politics in my *life*. I didn't have any idea that guys like this even watch sports. But apparently they do. And here we are now, and this was the result, and we have to deal with the reality of that. Right?

KENT. Right.

RAUL. And if you think about it, just bear with me here, if you really kind of think about it, it's not really such a bad thing, overall, from the biggest, like, point of view, because the point here is to educate people, right? Because, you know, we're role models, and so this is an opportunity to make sure some young kid who maybe looks up to me, or to you, or to whoever, who's in there, doesn't try to emulate a behavior that we know to have certain risks. And which also? Is questionable ethically.

KENT. *(beat)* What?

RAUL. What? What.

KENT. In your book you say that everyone should do it in order for us to reach the full limits of human potential and kind of dismiss the health risks as not relevant under proper supervision.

RAUL. Right, well –

KENT. And you don't really seem interested in the ethics at all.

RAUL. Well, right, but, yeah, but –

KENT. But?

RAUL. Well, you know, things change. The book came out a while ago.

KENT. It came out a month ago.

RAUL. And I have since then backed away from the positions you just mentioned.

KENT. Oh, I see. And you did that on the advice of a lawyer, or – ?

RAUL. Look, is there something you want to say to me?

KENT. Well I –

RAUL. Because if there is then I wish that you just say it, okay?

KENT. Okay. Well –

RAUL. But, wait wait, so, wait, hold on. You, uh, you read it?

KENT. What?

RAUL. The, you know –

KENT. Oh. Yeah, Raul. I, um. I did read parts of it. Yes.

RAUL. So, uh… What'd you think?

KENT. *What?*

RAUL. No, just –

KENT. Um. I thought the description of taking me into a bathroom stall and injecting fluid into my buttocks with a syringe was not totally necessary.

(*beat*)

RAUL. Right, well, the thing with that is –

KENT. Um, okay, look, I'm not mainly concerned with what you tried to do to me or what you said about me, okay? That doesn't really bother me, because I can rise above personal attacks and slander and whatever you want to call it because that isn't the kind of thing that I like to clutter up my mind with. That's not even what this is about for me as far as I'm concerned because unlike *some* people I am not always all the time just about me and how things are going to affect me personally. What I want to say to you is. Do you even realize what you have done to the game of baseball? To this thing that gave you everything you have in your life? To everybody that plays it, and to all the fans that love it, with this toxic bullshit of yours? Do you even realize?

(*beat*)

RAUL. I'm sorry. Bullshit?

KENT. What.

RAUL. Well we can talk about what I did or I didn't realize if you want, Kent, but first off I'm gonna have to hold you up there from calling it bullshit.

KENT. What else would you like me to call it.

RAUL. Well, it's the truth, Kent. However else you feel like you want to react to it, that's fine, but what I put in that book is the truth, so, I'm confused, maybe because, as you like to remind me, maybe cause I'm not exactly the brightest penny in the fountain over here, but isn't that the exact *opposite* of bullshit? Kent? *(beat)* Wait, what are you planning to say?

KENT. What?

RAUL. When they ask you. What are you gonna say?

(beat)

KENT. I'm –

RAUL. Holy shit. You're gonna lie.

KENT. No –

RAUL. You're gonna lie. You're gonna lie to fucking Congress.

KENT. *(overlapping)* I'm, no, I'm not –

RAUL. They make you take an oath in there. You know that right?

KENT. Yes. I know that.

RAUL. Well, so, then –

KENT. I'm not going to lie under oath, Raul.

RAUL. Okay. Good. But so… *(beat)* Oh. Right. So you've, uh, you've got one of those vague answers, right? That's not a lie but that doesn't so much answer the question either. Right? I'm right, right?

KENT. Everybody thinks you're full of shit.

RAUL. See? You're doing it already. That's not an answer to my question.

KENT. *Everybody.* Thinks you're full of shit.

RAUL. Everybody *wants* to think I'm full of shit. That's not the same.

KENT. We'll they're *saying* it.

RAUL. I don't care.

KENT. Tony says you're full of shit.

RAUL. I don't care.

KENT. Even Adam says you're full of shit.

RAUL. What? Who?

KENT. Um. Adam?

RAUL. Rook said that?

KENT. To the press. In Colorado.

RAUL. *(beat)* Why did he say it to the press in Colorado?

KENT. Because he lives in Colorado.

RAUL. *(beat)* Why does he live in Colorado?

KENT. That's…! Because he's their batting coach! That's –

RAUL. Whoa. Rook's coaching now? *Man.* That really –

KENT. That's not my – !

RAUL. I know. I know it's not –

KENT. That's not my point.

RAUL. *(overlapping)* It's not your point. I know that.

KENT. My *point* –

RAUL. You're point seems to be that everybody's afraid to tell the truth but me.

KENT. No –

RAUL. Well that is what it seemed to be.

KENT. Well it wasn't.

RAUL. Well then I missed it.

KENT. Would you let me – !

RAUL. No. Because I don't give a shit *what* that little back-stabbing faggot said to the press because, just like everybody else in the whole entire world, that kid always *worshipped* you, for absolutely no reason at all that I could understand, and so of *course* he's gonna have your back, and so I don't give a shit. *Come on!* The fuck *is* this, Kent? You start to believe your own hype? You even fooling *yourself* now? I mean, you want to try to duck and weave once you're inside there on the spot then that's your call, but can you even *say* it?

KENT. What.

RAUL. To me, here in this room, can you even say it out loud?

KENT. *What.*

RAUL. That you did it! That it happened!

KENT. Keep your voice down.

RAUL. Who the fuck are you *talking* to, Kent? I was there! I did it with you! I already know! Just say it! Say it! Say it motherfucker!

(KENT grabs RAUL. Slams him up against the wall. A moment.)

RAUL. Go ahead. What are you waiting for? Take a swing. I'll *let* you. I'll even let you. Take it. Free shot. *(pause)* The fuck are you *waiting* for? Bring it, brother. Bring it, Superman. Fucking bring it.

(pause)

KENT *Fuck!*

(KENT lets RAUL drop to the ground. Turns. Walks a few steps away. RAUL brushes off his suit, straightens his tie. A moment.)

KENT. Do you have any more of those?

RAUL. What? *(beat)* Oh. Yeah. Sure.

(RAUL hands KENT the bottle of pills and the water. KENT takes a pill. Hands the bottles back. Takes a deep breath. A moment.)

KENT. It is fucked up that you did this to me. It is so totally fucked up.

RAUL. Okay I didn't do anything *to* you –

KENT. *(overlapping)* Because it's not my fault that you squandered your talent. It's not my fault that I worked harder. It's not my fault you got hurt over and over and over again. None of those things are my fault.

RAUL. That's not it.

KENT. Then what is it?

RAUL. It's, what I said, it's for the game, for, you know, the *kids* –

KENT. *(overlapping)* That's, don't give me that, that is crap, why, *really?*

RAUL. *(overlapping)* No, because it's, I – !

KENT. Why the *fuck?*

RAUL. I don't know! I, uhhh…! *(pause)* I don't know. I don't.

KENT. Well that's…even worse.

RAUL. I mean, I'm professional athlete…

KENT. *(beat)* Is that supposed to be some kind of explanation?

RAUL. Just. We don't –

KENT. And, I mean, you couldn't have *waited?*

RAUL. What?

KENT. You couldn't at least have *waited,* oh, I don't know, three more years?

RAUL. Why?

KENT. You couldn't have fucking *waited* until 2007.

RAUL. Oh! Oh. Yeah, I guess not.

KENT. Well. That's just great.

RAUL. Come on. You think it's gonna make a *difference?* You think your eligibility's gonna come up, *you,* and anybody's gonna say a goddamn thing? No. They're gonna look the other way, and talk about the benefit of the doubt, and vote you right into the Hall, they –

KENT. But…! Don't you…! (pause) Of course everybody's afraid but you.

(Pause. **KENT** *looks at the door. He hesitates.)*

RAUL. What do you think they're gonna do?

KENT. To me?

RAUL. To *you?* Listen to this guy. Once he gets going… No, not to you, you fuck. To baseball.

KENT. Oh. Um. Nothing, probably. I mean, they'll make some recommendations, some demands, whatever, more testing, stiffer penalties, but what's the government really gonna do? Stop the season? Shut us down? Without baseball… Okay, what, Raul, what is so funny?

(Because **RAUL** *has started chuckling.)*

RAUL. No, no, nothing, just… "Stiffer penalties." Sorry.

KENT. Yeah that's great.

RAUL. Sorry. *(pause)* Hey, so, what's it gonna be?

KENT. What? What.

RAUL. Your vague answer.

KENT. Oh. It's, uh. It's, "I'm not here to talk about the past."

RAUL. Good. That's good.

KENT. And sometimes. "I'm not here to talk about the past. I'm here to be positive about this subject."

RAUL. Lawyers, man. *(beat)* Mine told me? With my book? That I should, like, change some names, leave some things vague, but, I was like: Fuck That. This Is America. Sue me, bitches. *(pause)* Look. This'll be done quick I bet. They got other work to do, these guys, some other committee, agriculture…whatnot. Something about…endangered species, or…farms… *(beat)* Hey! After this whole thing is over you want to maybe grab a game?

KENT. *What?*

RAUL. Just. D.C.'s got a team now. Ever since the Expos folded and came down from Montreal? I've never seen them play.

KENT. Um. I don't think so, Raul.

RAUL. Hey, okay. *(pause)* George W. Bush said to me once, he said to me one time: "What does Canada need with baseball teams anyway? It's ours. They've got hockey."

KENT. *(beat)* What?

RAUL. Yeah. Funny. He's right, though. I played in Toronto for a while? They don't know what to do with baseball up there. They sing the wrong National anthem before the game. I mean. Not the *wrong* one. Theirs. But it's weird.

KENT. You know the president?

RAUL. I played for him, Kent. When I was in Texas? He owned the team.

KENT. Oh yeah. *(beat)* Bill Clinton called me once.

RAUL. Yeah?

KENT. Yeah. When I hit 62. When I broke the record. Just to say hey.

RAUL. Huh. What a couple of pricks, right?

KENT. Seriously. What a pair of fucking pricks.

RAUL. Two total douchebags.

KENT. Just this duo of ridiculous unrepentant sacks of crap.

RAUL. Yeah. *(pause)* Hey, I heard you got married again.

KENT. Oh. Um. Yeah. Yes. I did.

RAUL. That's nice.

KENT. Yeah it is. She's great.

RAUL. What does she do?

KENT. She, uh. She's, um. *(beat)* She's a pharmaceuticals representative.

RAUL. Nice.

KENT. I heard you got divorced. Again.

RAUL. Yeah. Can't really. Can't seem to stick one of those out.

KENT. Looks that way.

RAUL. What can I say? I love women.

KENT. Raul, you hate women. It's a subtle difference.

RAUL. Look, I'm just trying to –

KENT. What.

RAUL. I don't know. *(pause)* Adam's *coaching*?

KENT. Adam's been retired five years. Some new kid came up on his club. Took Rookie of the Year at his position. They tried to move him but... He was done.

   (pause)

RAUL. Okay, see, when I met you? You were this hot prospect, California All-American, six foot a thousand, but you're coming up for the first time, so you've got that look all the rooks have, that wild-eyed look, are they gonna find me out, *that* look, and I –

KENT. What. You what. You 'took me under your *wing*'– ?

RAUL. No.

KENT. You *made* me, is *that* it?

RAUL. No –

KENT. Are you giving me *that* speech now? Because that is bullshit.

RAUL. No. Yes. It is.

KENT. Because I broke the rookie record for home runs.

RAUL. I know.

KENT. I walked onto the field with that. I didn't need you.

RAUL. Yeah. No. *(pause)* Yeah. Exactly.

KENT. What. *(pause)* What?

RAUL. You didn't need me. You never did. And you used me anyway.

KENT. I "used" you?

RAUL. And then I came back a few years later, when I was the one in real trouble, I was the one everybody was giving up on, and you used me again!

KENT. Oh *come on!* You *loved* being that guy! You *loved* that! You *loved* it!

RAUL. Maybe. Maybe I did. I don't care. All I know is? That after that? Every time I saw you, or heard your name, or read it in print? I wanted to take an aluminum bat? And beat you to death with it. And then I did the book? And I felt better. So, look, I know what everybody's saying and what they think and they can go ahead and they can do that. But all this really happened. And you *know* it. And Tony knows it. And fucking *Adam* knows it. And when you go talk to Congress? You hypocrite? Oh, yeah, I picked that one up along the way. When you go in there, you ingrate? You spoiled brat? You pathetic fucking crybaby? When you lean into the mic and tell them you're not here to talk about the past because you're just here to be positive about this subject, when you say that, over and over and over again? Everybody else will know it too.

(Long pause. **KENT** *goes to the door. Stops. Perhaps*

ADAM *is already visible now, beginning the next transition.)*

*(***KENT*** *goes.* **RAUL** *remains alone. Then,* **RAUL** *follows* **KENT** *off.)*

ADAM. Ready? Here comes the next one.

(And suddenly the space opens and for the first time we are actually on a baseball diamond. In the center. On the mound. **ADAM** *is here. He is dressed as before. There is a bucket of balls by his feet and he is holding a ball in his hand.)*

*(***ADAM*** *pitches. Watches a grounder.)*

ADAM. Come on. The fuck is that? You gotta get down on it, swing down, you're coming over the top, hitting it on the ground. Don't get me wrong, you've got good speed, but we don't want you having to leg it out all the time. Okay? Okay. Here we go.

*(***ADAM*** *grabs another ball and pitches. Watches a pop-up.)*

ADAM. Great. Now you're under it. Now you're under it too far and you popped it up and the inning is over and we lost. Come on. Show it to me.

*(***ADAM*** *grabs another ball and pitches. The batter misses entirely.)*

ADAM. Hey! Okay. Who are you? Are you the right guy? Are you the same guy I read the scouting report on? Cause I gotta tell you that this doesn't seem like the same guy to me. First of all you're watching yourself. I am watching you watch yourself. You're up in your head, thinking, here I am, this is it, I'm in the majors, let me put on a big show, let put on a show for Coach Adam, and you gotta forget that, and just take your time. Take your own time. Step out of the box, knock dirt off your cleats, spin the bat, and then step back in, to *your* rhythm, because you're only as good as this game, you're only as good as this at-bat, what you do right now, forget everything before, forget about that last pitch, even if you missed it, like you did, like some kind of bush league chump, forget it, and just step in for the next one, like it's the first. Okay?

(**ADAM** *pitches. Watches one lined past him to one side.*)

ADAM. There it is, rook. Now you're down on it. That's a base hit. I mean, not if *I'm* in the infield, but mostly, you're on, you moved somebody over, you drove somebody in. Now forget that one. Step in for this. This one is the only one there is.

(**ADAM** *pitches. Ducks as one is ripped back up the middle.*)

ADAM. Whoa! Don't hurt me now, rook. Don't hurt me. Okay. One more.

(**ADAM** *pitches. Spins around as a long drive is launched over him.*)

ADAM. There it is! There it is! On the screws! Now we're talking! Woo! *(He claps.)* Back…back…back…!

(**ADAM** *spins to face the batter. His expression is melancholy as all hell. A moment.*)

(*Blackout.*)

End of Play

Also by
Itamar Moses...

Bach At Leipzig

The Four of Us

Outrage

Please visit our website **samuelfrench.com** for complete
descriptions and licensing information

OTHER TITLES AVAILABLE FROM SAMUEL FRENCH

DEAD CITY
Sheila Callaghan

Full Length / Comic Drama / 3m, 4f / Unit Set
It's June 16, 2004. Samantha Blossom, a chipper woman in
her 40s, wakes up one June morning in her Upper East Side
apartment to find her life being narrated over the airwaves
of public radio. She discovers in the mail an envelope ad-
dressed to her husband from his lover, which spins her raw
and untethered into an odyssey through the city...a day full
of chance encounters, coincidences, a quick love affair, and a
fixation on the mysterious Jewel Jupiter. Jewel, the young but
damaged poet genius, eventually takes a shine to Samantha
and brings her on a midnight tour of the meat-packing dis-
trict which changes Samantha's life forever—or doesn't. This
90 minute comic drama is a modernized, gender-reversed,
relocated, hyper-theatrical riff on the novel *Ulysses*, occurring
exactly 100 years to the day after Joyce's jaunt through Dub-
lin.

"Wonderful...Sheila Callaghan's pleasingly witty and theatrical
new drama that is a love letter to New York masquerading as
hate mail...[Callaghan] writes with a world-weary tone and has a
poet's gift for economical description.
The entire dead city comes alive..."
- *The New York Times*

"*Dead City*, Sheila Callaghan's riff on James Joyce's *Ulysses* is
stylish, lyrical, fascinating, occasionally irritating, and emi-
nently worthwhile...the kind of work that is
thoroughly invigorating."
- *Back Stage*

SAMUELFRENCH.COM

OTHER TITLES AVAILABLE FROM SAMUEL FRENCH

JACK GOES BOATING
Bob Glaudini

Full Length / Comedy / 2m, 2f / Interior
Four flawed but likeable lower/middle-class New Yorkers interact in a touching and warm-hearted play about learning how to stay afloat in the deep water of day-to-day living. Laced with cooking classes, swimming lessons and a smorgasbord of illegal drugs, *Jack Goes Boating* is a story of date panic, marital meltdown, betrayal, and the prevailing grace of the human spirit.

"An immensely likable play [that] exudes a wry compassion."
- *The New York Times*

"Endearing romantic comedy about a married couple and the social-misfit friends they fix up. Witty and knowing and all heart."
- *Variety*

"Glides effortlessly from the shallow end of the emotional pool to the deep end."
- *Theatremania.com*